COFFEE AS IT IS,

AND

AS IT OUGHT TO BE.

By P. L. SIMMONDS.

MANY YEARS A COFFEE PLANTER IN JAMAICA,

And Editor of the Colonial Magazine; Honorary and Corresponding Member of the leading Agricultural and Commercial Societies of the British and Foreign Colonies.

LONDON:

Effingham Wilson, Royal Exchange.

1850

" Now stir the fire, and close the shutters fast,
Let fall the curtains, wheel the sofa round,
And, while the bubbling and loud-hissing urn
Throws up a steamy column, and the cups,
That cheer, but not inebriate, wait on each,—
So let us welcome peaceful ev'ning in."

Cowper's ' Task..'

LONDON :
PRINTED BY EFFINGHAM WILSON, ROYAL EXCHANGE.

PREFACE.

I MAY be permitted to state, that the ground-
work of the following little Treatise is an essay
read at the *conversaziones*, or evening meet-
ings, of several literary and scientific societies
in the provinces, some years ago; and which,
at the instigation of many of my friends,
and the request of my publisher, I have been
induced to amplify and revise for publica-
tion, now that the subject of which it treats
is attracting a more than common share of
public attention, in the hope that it may
prove interesting and useful.

P. L. SIMMONDS.

5, BARGE YARD, CITY,
May, 1850.

SUMMARY OF CONTENTS.

	Page.
Preface	3
Introductory Remarks on the extensive Adulteration of Coffee	5
Recent Memorial from the Merchants of London to the Lords of the Treasury	7
Substitution of Chicory for Coffee	8
Manufacture, Growth, and general Use of Chicory	12
Chemical Tests of Adulteration.	19
Other Substances used for Admixture and as Substitutes for Coffee	21
Chemical Opinions and Properties of Coffee	22
Comparison between the Consumption of the United States and Europe	28
Comparative Rates of Duty levied	30
Production and Consumption in various Countries	32
General Directions	34
Distinctive Character and Appearance of the Berries	36
Instructions for Roasting Coffee	41
Various Modes of making Coffee	47
Coffee as made in France	60
Coffee as drank in Turkey	67
System of Cultivating the Coffee Tree	70

COFFEE, AS IT IS,

AND

AS IT OUGHT TO BE.

No ARTICLE, it has been well observed, presents greater facility for adulteration than coffee; from its being usually purchased in a pulverized form. Its colour, too, is favourable to this; and its aroma being powerful, will bear a good deal of " taking down," without its deterioration being made very perceptible, unless to a practised dealer. In the continental towns, few buy coffee in its powdered form, except the humbler class of those who use it, or the indolent among the better sort; and the care of roasting the beans and grinding is thought by many masters of families too delicate and impor- tant a task to be entrusted by them to any servant. In this country, the adulteration of coffee has in- creased to an enormous extent, so as to retard the introduction of genuine coffee from abroad. The prin- cipal substances used for admixture are chicory, or the root of the dandelion, half-carbonized horse-beans pounded, roasted rye, and browned crusts grated down; but there are dozens of other ingredients had recourse to by unscrupulous and fraudulent venders. About thirty-six millions of pounds of genuine coffee are consumed yearly in the United Kingdom; and it is estimated that not less than eighteen million pounds more of vegetable matter of various kinds are sold under the name of coffee. Two-thirds at least of these eighteen million pounds of pretended coffee are composed of chicory, and the remaining third of other ingredients which are positively injurious to health, and a fraud upon the revenue.

In various parts of the metropolis, but more especially in the east, are to be found liver-bakers. These men take the livers of oxen and horses; bake them and grind them into a powder, which they sell to the low-priced coffee-shopkeepers, at from fourpence to sixpence per pound; horses'-liver coffee bearing the highest price. It may be known by allowing the coffee to stand until cold, when a thick pellicle or skin will be found on the top. It goes farther than coffee, and is generally mixed with chicory, and other vegetable imitations of coffee.

A MEMORIAL, numerously signed by the leading merchants of London, was forwarded in April, 1850, to the Lords of the Treasury, setting forth the gross adulteration practised in the article of coffee by the fraudulent and deleterious mixture of roasted acorns, chesnuts, peas and beans, red pottery earth, sand, mahogany saw-dust, colouring matter and finings, as also chicory. It is shown that a severe loss to the revenue accrues by the very serious and progressive diminution in the deliveries of coffee during the last few years, arising from the extensive adulteration spoken of, whilst considerable injustice is done to the coffee-planter, the fair trader, and the consumer. The object of the memorialists is not to prevent the fair, legitimate sale of chicory; but to prevent the sale of a mixture of coffee and chicory (or other substances) under the name of coffee; the former paying a heavy duty and the latter, if home-grown, paying none. They, therefore, pray that their lordships will rescind the order of August, 1840, sanctioning, contrary to the Act of Parliament of 43rd Geo. III., cap. 129, the fraudulent mixture of vegetable substances with coffee. From the great respectability of the memorialists, including the names of Messrs. Baring Brothers; Forbes and

Co.; Frederick Huth and Co.; Arbuthnot and Co.; Crawford, Colvin and Co.; Suse and Sibeth; and other leading houses, it is to be expected that the justice of their complaints will receive due attention from their lordships.

The serious and progressive diminution which has taken place in the consumption of coffee, may be seen by a reference to the following figures. In 1847 the deliveries for home consumption in the

United Kingdom, were . . . 37,472,153 lbs.
In 1848, they were . . . . 37,107,279 „
In 1849, they were . . . . 34,431,074 „ .

Whilst, in the first three months of the present year, duties have been paid in the five principal ports of Great Britain, on 5,888,761 lbs. against 7,623,464 lbs. in the corresponding period of 1849; thus showing, in addition to the already enormous diminution of revenue for 1849, a further decrease, in three months, of about £36,000.

Substitution of Chicory for Coffee.

In a Parliamentary paper recently printed, I find memorials from the Chamber of Commerce of Ceylon, and from planters and merchants connected with the coffee trade of that fine island, to the Lords of the Treasury, which contain facts and figures requiring deep consideration, and some few of which I shall cite, for more general publicity.

" From the information obtained by the Chamber of Commerce on the trade in chicory, it appears that the quantity retailed in its own name is very small, whilst the quantity mixed with coffee, in a ground state, is not less than one-third of the entire amount of coffee consumed in the kingdom.

" From the official returns of the Honourable the Board of Trade, it appears that the quantity of coffee entered for home consumption in 1848, was 37,186,292 lbs., from which it might be calculated that the quantity of chicory consumed was 12,368,764 lbs., equal to 5,521 tons, probably considerably under the actual consumption, which has lately been calculated by Mr. M'Culloch and other competent judges in England to be about 12,500 tons per annum.

" Presuming that this quantity of chicory has replaced an equal quantity of coffee, consisting of British plantation and foreign, in proportion to the relative quantities of each actually consumed, it would give, on the lower calculation, 10,048,902 lbs. British plantation, and 2,379,862 lbs. foreign;

and, on the higher calculation, 22,743,873 lbs.
British plantation, and 5,251,627 lbs. foreign;
the duty on which would have amounted to
£225,478 in the former, and £510,430 in the
latter case."

" Your memorialists have been made aware,
through their commercial correspondents in the
United Kingdom, that the growth and consumption of chicory, the whole of which is sold in
Great Britain in the form of coffee, has increased
to a very considerable extent; that the estimated
production of 6,720,000 lbs. in 1842, must have
more than doubled since that time.

" Your memorialists trace the cause of this
alarming increase in the fraudulent use of this
article to the relaxations of the wholesome and
judicious Excise regulations under 3 Geo. IV.,
cap. 53, by which dealers in coffee were prohibited,
under a penalty of £50, from selling or having on
their premises any vegetable substance for the
purpose of mixing with coffee. On the first introduction of chicory into Great Britain, a nominal
duty of 20 per cent. was levied upon it, which,
owing to the representations of the trade, was
afterwards increased to the same rate as that then
payable on British plantation coffee. But the

subsequent cultivation of the plant in England, of which it is the prepared root, from which no duty is derived, has rendered nugatory the expectations formed from that measure, of justice to the coffee growers and traders. Chicory can now be delivered to the wholesale dealers at $2\frac{1}{4}d.$ per lb., whilst the duty-paid prices of coffee range from $8d.$ to $1s.$ $1\frac{1}{2}d.$ per lb. ; the temptation to its fraudulent use, therefore, is obviously great, and against which there is no penal restriction.

" In the absence of any official returns, or means of ascertaining the quantity of chicory grown and consumed in the United Kingdom, your memorialists cannot state, with the accuracy which they could wish, the extent to which the revenue from coffee suffers by the use of the adulterating ingredient. But they have learned from colonial brokers, and gentlemen of experience largely connected with the coffee trade, as well as from the testimony of the most experienced officers of the Excise, that of the large proportion of coffee retailed to the poorer classes in a ground state, sometimes one-third, and in many instances one half, is composed of adulterating ingredients. It is also notorious, that the finer descriptions of Ceylon coffee, Java, and Costa Rica (a foreign coffee of great strength and flavour, recently introduced), receive a marked preference in the market, by reason of their quality of bearing a greater admixture of chicory.

" Your memorialists, therefore, humbly submit that if the sale of chicory were again, in conformity with the Act 3 Geo. IV., cap. 53, restricted to persons not being venders of coffee, and consumers were left to make their own mixture of these ingredients, that the result would be a proportionate increase in the consumption of the genuine article, to the extent of 6,000,000 lbs., or fully one-half of the supposed quantity of coffee displaced in consumption, by the fraudulent sale of adulterating compounds; which, in the present proportionate quantities consumed of British plantation and foreign coffee, would yield an increase of revenue equal to £116,000, and a corresponding benefit to the import merchant and colonial producer, by relieving the market of the same additional quantity of coffee."

Manufacture, Growth, and general Use of Chicory.

The manufacture of a factitious coffee from the roasted root of chicory, the wild endive *(Cichorium intybus)* of our fields, appears to have originated in

Holland, where it has been practised for more
than a century. It remained a secret until 1801,
when it was introduced into France by M. Orban
of Liege, and M. Giraud of Homing, a short dis-
tance from Valenciennes.

In Holland chicory is mixed, in variable proportions, with coffee; the resulting product is very
bitter, which is considered by the common people
to be a most salutary refreshment, which modifies
the stimulant action of the coffee. Such a favourable idea has been formed of it, that of late this
preparation has been employed alone, without any
addition of coffee; and, nevertheless, it possesses
no other virtue than that of colouring, more or less
readily, the water in which it is boiled or infused;
of communicating to the liquid the bitter taste of
the extractive substances contained in chicory; and
of being far less expensive than coffee.

The manufacture of chicory-coffee, however, remained for a long time stationary and of little
importance; but for the last twenty years it has
extended considerably, and become an object of
commerce of great importance. Till within the
last few years it was carried on principally near
Valenciennes; but since then manufactories have
sprung up in several localities, especially at Arras,

B

Cambray, Lille, Paris, Senlis in Normandy, Brittany, Jersey and Guernsey, and in England. The English counties where it is chiefly grown are Yorkshire, Leicestershire, Cambridge, Suffolk, and latterly Kent. Chicory was recommended, many years ago, by Arthur Young, as a forage plant, and is extensively grown for this purpose on the continent; but it gives a bad taste to the milk of the cows which feed on it.

The cultivation of chicory, to obtain the root for the purpose of converting it into coffee, has become a source of great prosperity for these districts. The plant requires a deep soil of good quality, and well prepared: the seed, about 13lbs. to the acre, is sown in May, and the harvest takes place in October. Sometime before collecting the roots the leaves are mowed, and cows fed upon them. The roots are dug up with a spade, placed in heaps, and covered with straw, to preserve them from frost.

The roots, thus collected, are cut at first longitudinally, and then transversely, in several pieces; they are then carried into the drying chambers, which are heated with a kind of anthracite, producing no smoke. The roots are placed in layers; they are frequently stirred, to prevent them from burning, and to facilitate the drying. Four such operations are made in about twenty-four hours. The roots, dried by the above process, are known by the name of *cossètes*. They are kept in granaries; but, in general, sold almost immediately to the manufacturers, who roast them according to the demand. When the roasting is nearly complete, 2 per cent. of butter is added, and a couple of turns given to the roasting-machine. This addition is made, in order to impart lustre to the chicory, and to give it the appearance of roasted coffee. The substance is then emptied into iron vessels, and, after cooling, is crushed in vertical stone mills or between iron cylinders; it is then sifted; and during this operation a small quantity of reddish colouring substance is added, to give it the colour of coffee. The product is then weighed off, and sold in packets, under a variety of names, but very rarely under its own; for instance, among others, Mocha powder, ladies' coffee, cream of Mocha, pectoral coffee, Chinese coffee, Tom Thumb coffee, Polka coffee, and colonial coffee.

I have stated that it forms a very important object of commerce; in fact, about 12,000,000 pounds are consumed yearly. On consulting the tables of the commerce of France, I find that, from 1827 to 1836, there were exported from France 458,971 kilogrammes (about one million pounds) of chicory-coffee, of the value of 321,282 francs; and since this period the amount has vastly increased.

Latterly, says Mr. M'Culloch, chicory has been largely substituted for coffee here, as well as on the continent; and as foreign chicory, when imported, pays a duty of 4½d. per pound, while that raised at home pays no duty, its cultivation has been rapidly extended. It has, in fact, been affirmed by those best acquainted with the subject, that in 1842, the growth of British chicory was little, if at all, short of 3000 tons. We need not, therefore, be surprised, considering the influence of this large and rapidly increasing supply of untaxed chicory over the consumption of coffee, and the revenue derived from it, that the subject has engaged a good deal of attention. If a duty is to be laid on coffee, the interests of the consumer and of the revenue alike require that an equal duty should be laid on all articles used either as substitutes for coffee, or (which is the usual method of employing chicory) as a means of adulterating the latter. The substitution of chicory for coffee has already occasioned a loss to the revenue of many

hundred thousands of pounds sterling a year, besides its mischievous influence in adulterating and
debasing a popular beverage.

But it is not the admixture of chicory alone of
which there is cause to complain. Mr. Samuel
Younger, a large importer, who first introduced
the root to notice in this country, in 1834, asserts,
in a memorial to the Lords of the Treasury last
year, that the English farmer, not content with
the large protection of £20 per ton and 5 per
cent. duty (which the foreign root has to pay),
adulterates chicory considerably. His words are
well worth recording.

" Many of the growers, hearing that the chicory
root was adulterated by many of the manufacturers, and seeing that the article must be kiln-
dried, to fit it for market, at once hit upon the
plan of adulterating the chicory root themselves,
to the extent of never less than 25 per cent., and
frequently 50 per cent., by adding other roots,
prepared in the same way, which, when kiln-dried,
curl up and assume the same appearance as the
chicory root; such as the parsnip, the white carrot, the beet-root, the radish, or any such answer-
ing the purpose.

" My Lords have now only to suppose a parcel

of English chicory root prepared in this way for
sale, for which the full price is given, and bought
by a respectable house, whose principle of trade is
to go with the times, or, in other words, not to
lose their chance in the throng for want of doing
as others do. The parcel of chicory root bought
by this respectable house is forthwith adulterated
with pulse to the extent of sometimes 25 per cent.,
sometimes 50, and sometimes 75 per cent., which
amount of adulteration is governed entirely by the
price at which orders may be obtained, this respectable house manufacturing it into every variety
of quality, to answer the price at which their
travellers require it for their customers.

" Suppose the manufacturer reduces this com-
modity only 25 per cent., it is clear that the article
offered for sale as chicory powder contains only 50
per cent. of chicory, the farmer having already
reduced it 25 per cent.; but if the farmer has
mixed other roots with the chicory root, to the
extent of 50 per cent., it is self-evident, that by
the time it gets into the possession of the grocer,
the identity of chicory cannot be traced—it is lost."

The possession of substances for adulterating
coffee was formerly an offence punishable by the
forfeiture of the articles and a penalty of £100.

But by the Act of 3rd Geo. IV., cap. 53, persons who are *not dealers in coffee* may obtain a license for roasting and selling corn, peas, beans, or parsnips, labelling the parcels with the names, and conforming to the various regulations prescribed in the Act. Dealers in coffee are obliged to take out a license, renewable annually, which at present costs 11s.

Chemical Tests of Adulteration.

Chicory is detected by shaking the suspected article with cold water, in a tumbler or glass vessel; if the coffee be pure, it will swim and give little or no colour to the liquid; but if chicory be present, it sinks to the bottom, and communicates a pretty deep red tint to the water. The presence of this root may also be assumed by finding it sticky on the fingers, and running into little balls, when mixed up with water. The particles of coffee are *grouty*, as some significantly call them—that is, granular; and have, therefore, small tendency to cohere. The gross fraud practiced on the public by the extensive use of chicory may be understood from the fact, that foreign chicory root is only one-third of the price of the best coffee, while chicory of British growth, having no import duty to pay, is necessarily cheaper still.

Roasted Corn, Haricots and Peas may be detected by adding tincture of iodine to a cold decoction of suspected coffee, which will produce a blue colour to the liquid.

Brick-dust, Ochre, and Earth may be detected by incineration and determining the amount of ash; 3 ounces of pure chicory coffee furnish from 4 to 5 per cent. of residue; an access would indicate fraud.

Adulteration with Coffee-grounds.—This is carried on upon a great scale in Paris. It is easily detected. A sample of the suspected chicory is dried in a water-bath, and a pinch thrown upon the surface of a glass of water; the chicory almost immediately absorbs the water, and sinks to the bottom of the vessel, whilst the coffee-grounds remain on the surface.

Adulteration with Roasted Bread, Dirt, and Remains from Vermicelli, &c.—This adulteration is generally made with crusts of bread collected in the streets; crusts which are not always very clean. They are roasted, or rather burnt, in the oven, ground, and mixed with the chicory-powder. This adulteration can be detected by iodine-water, as the product resulting from the decoction of pure chicory does not strike a blue colour.

Adulteration with Roasted Acorns, which may be detected by iodine-water and by persulphate of iron, which, in such a case, strikes a blue colour.

There is no method as yet known of detecting the adulteration by roasted beet-root and carrot.

Other Substances used for Admixture and as Substitutes for Coffee.

Amongst the vegetable substances which have been tried as substitutes for genuine coffee, or for admixture and adulteration, are Corsican coffee, made from the seeds of knee holly (*Ruscus aculeatus*); Rosetta coffee, from the seeds of fenugrek, adding a little lemon juice; Egyptian coffee, from chick pea (*Lathyrus sativus*); broom coffee, from its seeds; gooseberry and currant coffee, from the seeds washed out of the cake left after making wine from these fruits, as also from grape seeds; rice coffee, from the husked seeds. This is much esteemed by the lower classes in India, where it is sometimes found that these substitutes agree better than the Turkey coffee.

Rye coffee, known as Hunt's economical breakfast powder, from the grain, roasted along with a

little butter. The seeds of the yellow water-iris
(*Iris pseud-acorus*); this is considered one of the
best of the European substitutes. Acorns and
beet-root have also been used for this purpose.
In America and the West Indies the ripe seeds of
the ochro plant (*Abelmoschus esculentus*) are found
to be a very palatable ingredient.

The pods of *Astragulus bæticus* are in general
use under the name of Swedish coffee, in the north
of Europe.

The produce of any of these plants cannot,
however, compete with the genuine coffee-berry,
in aromatic or stimulating qualities ; and the cheap
price of coffee renders a resort to other substitutes
unnecessary in the present day; particularly as
the expense and labour necessarily attendant on
the production of these preparations would be
quite inadequate to the advantage thus obtained.

Chemical Opinions, and Properties of Coffee.

The analyses of several French chemists prove
that the berry of the coffee grown in Martinique
contains the largest proportion of the active principle or caffeine. The varieties of coffees may,

therefore, be classed in the following order, according to the relative quantity of caffeine they contain :—Martinique, Alexandria, Java, Mocha, Cayenne and St. Domingo. An infusion of coffee, in the proportion of one hundred grammes (rather more than three ounces) to a little water, contains twenty grammes of alimentary substance, being three times as much as would be the case with an infusion of tea in the same proportion.

M. Rayen, from elaborate experiments, shows that coffee slightly roasted is that which contains the maximum of aroma, weight and nutrition. He declares coffee to be very nutritious, as it contains a large quantity of azote, and more than twice the nourishment of soup (*bouillon*). Chicory contains only half the nutriment of coffee.

Coffee is one of the most powerful means, not only of rendering animal and vegetable effluvia innocuous, but of actually destroying them. A room in which meat in an advanced degree of decomposition had been kept for some time, was instantly deprived of all smell on an open coffee-roaster being carried through it, containing a pound of coffee newly roasted. In another room exposed to the effluvium occasioned by the

clearing out of a dung-pit, the stench was completely removed within half a minute, on the em-
ployment of three ounces of fresh-roasted coffee;
whilst the other parts of the house were perma-
nently cleared of the same smell by being simply
traversed with the coffee-roaster, although the
cleansing of the dung-pit lasted for several hours
longer. Even the smell of musk and castoreum,
which cannot be overpowered by any other substance, is completely dispelled by the fumes of
coffee; and the same applies to the odour of
assafœtida.

It is a fact not generally known, that a man
may be literally and truly electrified with newly-
ground coffee. The manner of doing so I witnessed very recently. A large coffee-mill, driven
by a steam-engine, was grinding coffee into a
huge barrel. In the barrel stood a copper scoop,
directly under the fall of the fresh-ground
coffee. An iron rod being held within an inch
or so of the copper scoop, an instantaneous
flash or stream of electric fluid was attracted by
the iron. The same result followed when the
finger was employed instead of the rod, and a
slight shock, like the puncture of a pin, was quite
perceptible. By a rude contrivance, a shock was

also communicated from the ground coffee to the tail of a cat, when off scampered the bewildered animal in a state of the most earnest astonishment. Altogether, the matter is curious, and not beneath the attention of the philosopher.

One of the most remarkable facts in the diet of mankind is the enormous consumption of coffee and tea. The slightly stimulating and narcotic properties of these substances do not seem sufficient to account for the fact, that upwards of 800 millions of pounds of these articles are annually consumed by the inhabitants of the world. The researches of chemists, however, have proved that they contain an active principle, which, though small in quantity, yet forms an important part in the human economy.

With regard to the action upon the animal economy of coffee, tea and cocoa, which contain this common chemical principle, called caffeine, theine, &c., Professor Liebig has lately advanced some ingenious views, and has in particular endeavoured to show that, to persons of sedentary habits, in the present refined state of society, they afford eminently useful beverages, which contribute to the formation of the characteristic principle of bile. This important secreted fluid, deemed

c

by Liebig to be subservient to the function of
respiration, requires for its formation much azot-
ised matter, and that in a state of combination
analogous to what exists in caffeine.

Pfaff obtained only 90 grains of caffeine from
six pounds of coffee beans. There is also an acid
in raw coffee, to which the name of caffeic acid
has been given.

The useful and agreeable matter in coffee is
very soluble ; it comes off with the first waters of
infusion, and needs no boiling.

Dr. Moseley observes, that the extraordinary
influence which coffee, judiciously prepared, im-
parts to the stomach, from its tonic and invigorat-
ing qualities, is strongly exemplified by the immediate effect produced on taking it when the stomach
is overloaded with food, nauseated with surfeit, or
debilitated by intemperance. To constitutionally
weak stomachs it affords a pleasing sensation ; it
accelerates the powers of digestion, corrects crudi-
ties, and removes colic and flatulencies. Besides
its effect in keeping up the harmony of the gastric
powers, it diffuses a genial warmth that cherishes
the animal spirits, and takes away the listlessness
and languor which so greatly embitter the hours
of nervous people, after any deviation to excess,

fatigue, or irregularity. In the West Indies, where violent species of headache are more frequent and more severe than in Europe, coffee is the only medicine that affords relief.

The too free use, or rather abuse, of coffee is said to produce feverish heat, anxiety, palpitations, trembling, weakness of the sight, and predisposition to apoplexy. The quality and effects of coffee, however, will differ according to the manner in which it is roasted. Musgrave and Percival recommend its use in asthma; indeed, most persons labouring under that distressing malady seem to derive benefit from its use.

Coffee should always be drank in the morning and tea at night; for the coffee, which is nutritious at breakfast, becomes a stimulus at night; and the tea, which acts as a diluent at night, gives nothing for support during the day,

The usual heat at which coffee is drank is 100°.

Coffee, which is at present one of the most important of foreign productions used for food, whether as regards quantity or amount of revenue derived, was originally of little consequence in the markets.

But such has been the working of the " sober

berry juice," that the production in different parts of the world has increased enormously; and the consumption of no article is now more general than the one which forms the subject of our present investigation.

It was given in evidence before the Committee on Import Duties, which sat in 1840, that since the duty on British plantation coffee was reduced to 4d. per lb., there have been a vast number of coffee-shops opened in London, at which working men are served at a low price; that some of these places are frequented daily by many hundreds of persons, who used formerly to resort for refreshment to public-houses; that this beneficial change in the habits of working-men has been entirely owing to the cheapness of the refreshment obtained; and that any advance in the price, which should remove this advantage of comparative cheapness, would have the effect of sending the present customers of coffee-shops back to the use of intoxicating liquors. The number of these shops in the metropolis is nearly one thousand.

Comparison between the Consumption of the United States and Europe.

The present annual consumption of coffee in

Europe and the United States is about 258 thousand tons or 578 millions of pounds; of which the latter consume 170 millions. The American population being twenty millions, and the European 250 millions, this consumption gives an average of 8½ pounds to each American, and less than 1½ to each European. The cause of this difference is found in the different conditions of the "masses" in the two continents. In the United States coffee is used by all persons, in town or country, agricultural, artisan, mercantile, professional. In Europe it is used only by the rich, or the trading and middle classes of society; not generally by the peasant or operative. But, as the improvement of the condition of the working classes, and the consequent elevation of the "masses," are rapidly proceeding in Europe, the consumption of coffee and all other domestic comforts may be expected to be as great, proportionally, in Europe, as in the United States. If these twenty millions of Americans now consume 170 millions of pounds, how many millions will 250 millions of Europeans consume in the same proportion? Only 2175 millions! This is about 1400 millions more than the present produce of Brazil, the East and West Indies, Arabia, and all

other countries producing coffee for Europe and
the United States. Here is certainly *some* scope
for increased foreign and colonial production.

Comparative Rates of Duty levied.

In the United States coffee is admitted free
of duty; hence, the consuming price is only about
5*d*. per ℔., while, in the United Kingdom, the
duty being 4*d*. on British plantation coffee, and
6*d* on that of foreign growth, the consuming price
is from 1*s*. to 1*s*. 8*d*. Coffee, when first introduced
into England about the middle of the seventeenth
century, was sold in a liquid state, and paid a
duty of 4*d*. *a gallon;* afterwards, until the year
1732, the duty was 2*s*. per pound; it was then
reduced to 1*s*. 6*d*.; since which it has paid various
rates of duty. Each of these reductions we find
marked by an immense increase in the consumption.

The quantities of coffee consumed in Great
Britain in each of the several years of the decennial census, comparing the consumption with the
growth of the population, and exhibiting the influence of high and low duties, are shown by the
following statement, given by Mr. Porter in his

" Progress of the Nation," to which I have added
a similar estimate for 1849.

Years.	No. of lbs. consumed.	Rate of duty per lb. on British plantation coffee.		Population of Great Britain.	Average consumption.		Sums contributed per head to Revenue.
		s.	d.		lbs.	ozs.	d.
1801	750,861	1	6	10,942,646	0	1·09	1¼
1811	6,390,122	0	7	12,596,803	0	8·12	4
1821	7,327,283	1	0	14,391,631	0	8·01	6
1831	21,842,264	0	6	16,262,301	1	5·49	8
1841	27.298,322	0	6	18,532,335	1	7·55	10½(?)
1849	34,431,074	0	4	20,000,000	1	11·50	7

It appears, from the above statement, that when
the duty amounted to 1s. 6d. per pound, the use of
coffee was confined altogether to the rich.   The
quantity used throughout the kingdom scarcely ex-
ceeded, on the average, one ounce for each inhabi-
tant in the year ; and the revenue derived was altogether insignificant.   In the interval between
1801 and 1811, the rate of duty was reduced from
1s. 6d. to 7d. per lb., whereupon the consumption
rose 750 per cent., and the revenue derived was
increased more than threefold.   During the next
decennary period the duty was again advanced to
1s. per lb. ; by which means the progressive increase was checked, so as to render the consump-

tion actually less in 1821, taking the increased population into account, than it was in 1811. It has since gone on increasing with the reduction of duty and progress of population.

In 1760, the total quantity of coffee consumed in the United Kingdom was 262,000 lbs., or three quarters of an ounce to each person in the population. In 1833, the quantity was 20,691,000 lbs., or a pound and a half to each person per annum. The consumption is now nearly a pound and three quarters to each individual.

It is a remarkable instance of the perversity of the human will, when left to itself, that while coffee, with all its singular powers of cheering the mind and refreshing the nerves, took nearly four hundred years to make itself known in Europe, tobacco took little more than half a dozen years to be known as far as ships could carry it.

Production and Consumption in various Countries.

The following figures will show the comparative production and consumption of coffee over the world in the years 1832, 1841, and 1845.

Production in Millions of Pounds.

	1832	1841	1845
Brazil	80·6	156·8	180·0
Java	40·3	112·0	100·0
Cuba and Porto Rico ..	56·0	56·0	25·0
St. Domingo	44·8	33·6	30·0
British West Indies....	24·6	13·4	12·0
Sumatra .... } Mocha, Bourbon, &c.. }	44·8	13·4 11·2	15·0 10·0
British India and Ceylon	6·7	6·7	10·0
French and Dutch West Indies ...... }	17·9	6·7	6·0
La Guayra and Porto Cabello .... }	13·4	22·4	20·0
	329·1	432·2	408·0

Consumption of the Chief Countries in Millions of Pounds.

	1832	1841	1845
Holland and the Netherlands .... }	90·7	112·0	125·0
Germany and North of Europe .... }	71·7	89·6	100·0
France and South of Europe .... }	78·4	89·6	95·0
Great Britain	23·5	33·6	40·0
United States ...... } British North American Provinces .... }	45·9	100·8 11·2	120·0 15·0
	310·2	436·8	495·0

General Directions.

The use of coffee has now become general, and, when prepared as a beverage on right principles, no dietetic drink deserves to be more highly esteemed, both from its grateful aroma and savour, and its essentially wholesome character, as well as from its being more likely than any other to supersede the baneful and lamentable use of spirituous liquors, and thus to advance, in the surest and most permanent way, the cause of order, morality and temperance. Any method, therefore, for preparing it in a superior way, and procuring it in such a state that it may be presented before the most fastidious coffee-drinker with the certainty that it will be relished, cannot but deserve to be generally known, especially when so much ignorance prevails on the matter, and when it is so exceedingly rare to meet with a cup of really good coffee.

The coffee-dealer may be as careful as he will in his efforts to produce a really good article for his customers, and yet, in its after preparation as a beverage, it may be completely robbed of all its essential and grateful qualities.

The question is often asked, why it is that good coffee cannot be procured in this country? The reason is simply this,—coffee is spoiled in the burning, and sufficient care is not taken in preparing it for the table.

I confess that I am a perfect epicure in this very delightful beverage; and, as I abominate the muddy mawkish rubbish which is too often administered, and take it for granted that others who may be similarly impressed with its nauseousness would be gratified to be informed of the most economical methods of obtaining the best coffee, I will proceed to instruct them in the most simple manner.

There are two kinds of the berry to which I would recommend my readers to restrict their choice—the Mocha, and the Plantation, or rather Berbice. There is a third, which is cheap, but very coarse-flavored—the Ceylon; but I repeat, that the two first-named are those to which I give the preference. To rigid economists, I would advise that Berbice only be purchased; but the flavour of the Mocha is so fine, that a portion should always be mixed with the Plantation.

Distinctive Character and Appearance of the Berries.

It is quite essential that buyers should be intimately acquainted with the appearance of the various berries ; because, although a grocer cannot adulterate the article in its raw state, he can deceive and pass off upon his uninitiated customers the worst, for the most approved kinds ; and this I know to be the case in many instances. They who have once seen the two berries or beans, Mocha and Plantation, can never be again deceived. As I cannot show, I will describe them. I speak of coffee in the raw state ; for, on every account, I would strenuously advise that my readers should purchase it unroasted. Mocha (or, as it is often called, Turkey) coffee is the smallest of all the usual sorts ; it is round, plump, rough, equal-sized, the colour inclining to buff, with a tinge of pale brown, or of a light olive hue ; the Jamaica, Plantation, Berbice (for they much resemble one another) are fine, large, flat, handsome-looking berries, with a hue of grey-green, very different from those of Mocha, or even of Ceylon ; which last, from similarity of colour, might deceive those who are not aware of this distinctive difference, namely, that the Ceylon berries are of irregular sizes, ill-shaped, and of a spotted, dirty cream colour. The grey-green shade of the western coffees is entirely deficient in those of Asia. In its raw state, this article of consumption, unlike other grains, such as rice, wheat, &c., appears to be entirely exempt from the destructive ravages of insects ; it will keep good, nay, perhaps, improve, for an indefinite length of time; and may, consequently, be purchased at any period and in any quantity, when an opportunity offers for obtaining it at a wholesale price. Roasted coffee, on the contrary, deteriorates rapidly; and, if exposed to the air, loses its aroma ; hence one of the causes that this beverage is so seldom good. Instead of being exposed, as we see it, in shops, it should be kept closely stopped in canisters, or wide-mouthed glass bottles. The sooner coffee is used after it is roasted, the finer will be its flavour; hence, I prefer to roast only the quantity intended for the consumption of one week.

The value of the coffee berry in the British markets is not a fictitious quality, as some imagine, but is real, and depends :—

First, upon the texture and form of the berry; secondly, the colour; and thirdly, the flavour.

The texture of the berry and form, termed "style" by the coffee-dealers, is so well defined and palpable to the initiated, that, at one view, they pronounce its value from 150 shillings downwards, according to the two other qualities, colour and flavour. This great distinction in price, like the higher flavoured and priced wines, is admitted by the consumers, who are chiefly to be found among the manufacturers and artisans, particularly at Manchester, Birmingham, and other large manufacturing towns.

The dealers admit that these high-priced coffees pay them much better than low and ordinary, as they can admix a larger proportion of chicory with the former, without deteriorating the article, and which the inferior will not allow.

There is a peculiarity of flavour in Demerara coffee, which the brokers and dealers call "unclean," "unsound," and which in the colony is termed "rank" flavoured, and is found peculiar to the new coffee, so that those who have the option, never drink coffee under one or two years old. Another term, or set of terms, deprecatory of some West India coffee, is "bricky," "earthy-flavoured," &c.,

which means the same as the former. All the commoner and condemned qualities give out, on roasting, a dense vapour with a strong rank smell; they open and swell, and lose more weight by six or eight per cent., than the fine qualities which have " style."

These latter give out a transparent blue vapour, in very small quantities, and with a fine aroma, and retain the form of the berry.

The colour of the fine Jamaica is a delicate, even pale-green, approaching to sea-green, without any blue mottles, as is observed in Demerara coffee. In roasting the inferior qualities, a number of white berries appear, instead of roasting brown. They have neither weight nor flavour.

A difference of £3 per cwt. between the best Jamaica and Demerara coffee renders it worth while to inquire how this difference arises, and how it may be equalized. Climate, situation, and atmosphere enter, no doubt, into the question; but soil, drainage, gathering only the full-ripe berries, pulping before fermentation takes place, and the subsequent washing in frequent and running waters, to carry off fetid odour (which otherwise arises from the coffee-water), and may be reasonably supposed to impart some of its nauseous flavour to a substance so sensitive and ready to imbibe foreign flavour as the coffee-berry, are most important. I have been assured that a coffee-planter in Venezuela, who has studied the subject, and closes his manufactory, in order to retain his secret, has recently doubled the value of his crop, by the mode of preparing and gathering it.

Next to Mocha, in European reputation, are the Martinique and Bourbon coffees; the former is larger than the Arabian, and more oblong; it is rounded at the ends; its colour is greenish, and it preserves almost always a silver grey pellicle, which comes off in the roasting. The Bourbon coffee approaches nearest to the Mocha, from which it originally sprung. The Saint Domingo coffee has its two extremities pointed, and is much less esteemed than the preceding. The berries ought to be of a middling size, clear, and plump. Good West India coffee should be of a greenish colour, fresh, and free from any unpleasant smell; the berries small and unbroken.

All coffee becomes yellow, and improves in flavour, with age; and hence, in most foreign countries, "old Java" is preferred to any other kind, next to Mocha. The coffee of Arabia, when it is indigenous, being produced on a very dry soil, under a burning sun, sooner loses its green colour and raw flavour than any other; and, therefore, more speedily acquires that perfect ripeness so necessary to develope the best flavour. The Dutch understand this, and keep the coffee of Java in store, till age makes it the *next best* in the world.

Instructions for Roasting Coffee.

The process of roasting coffee is very simple, and occupies but twenty minutes. I have heard that persons have actually cooked this Arabian dainty in a frying-pan, and smothered it in butter, to keep it from burning. " Oh, the pity of it!" Who can be surprised that the results of such an ungainly, antediluvian method should be otherwise than delightful. It is nearly as barbarous as serving up tea-leaves with melted butter, of which a story is somewhere told, instead of drinking the decoction.

In private families, where this beverage is taken once a day, a coffee-roaster must be provided, which will *contain* a pound of the raw berries, although only two-thirds of that quantity should

be put into it; as, in the operation of roasting,
they will swell to nearly one-third more than the
space they occupy when raw, and room must be
given them to move about and be well shaken,
during the process. These domestic utensils,
although not common, are to be purchased at any
furnishing ironmongers. They are of iron, cylindrical shaped, and of various sizes; those which
will contain a pound of raw coffee are about four
inches wide, and seven in length, with a small
sliding-door, also of iron, having a ledge by which
it can be opened and shut, by means of a pair of
pincers, or even by tapping it with any convenient article, such as a pocket-knife. In the
middle of this cylinder, at one end, is fixed an
iron handle, about eight inches long, and hollow,
into which a round wooden handle is fastened,
two feet in length. Having made a clear fire
below the *upper bar of the grate*, so as to admit of
the action of rolling the roaster backwards and
forwards along the top, without impediment, put
into the machine as much raw coffee as will rather
more than three parts fill it, and commence
roasting, by turning the handle quickly and inces-
santly, though not velociously. If this rotatory
motion be stopped, a snapping noise will be heard.

This is caused by the berries being unequally
roasted: those at the bottom will be burning,
while others are not exposed to any heat. The
rolling backwards and forwards, therefore, must
not be discontinued, except while another motion
is substituted, which is, to lift the roaster up now
and then, and shake it the contrary way, in order
more thoroughly to intermix and change the posi-
tion of the berries, so that the process may proceed equally. The great secret to obtain fine-
flavoured coffee is to prevent the escape of the
aroma; hence, the roaster should be opened as
seldom as possible; and, for a quarter of an hour,
it will be wholly unnecessary. As the process
draws to a close, however, it will be requisite to
investigate its progress; but this must be done
quickly. No kind of manual dexterity is acquired
at once; but practice will soon render this as
easy and certain as any other. On no account
must any butter or other extraneous matter be
introduced; coffee exudes an essential oil, which
will prove the best, as it must be the only, medium
in the process.

In a quarter of an hour the little door should
be opened, and the state of the berries inspected.
If they look brown, but of various shades, the

heat has not been equally disseminated; and the roaster must be well shaken for half a minute, and then replaced on a cooler part of the fire, on the top bar, to finish gradually, still being rolled and shaken alternately. As twenty minutes is the time in which a batch will be finished, with proper management, it must be looked at once or twice more; when the eye, as well as sense of smell, will soon acquire experience in deciding whether the operation is finished. It must now be taken off the fire; but, as there is naturally a great body of heat still remaining in the cylinder (sufficient, indeed, to burn the berries), it must not be left; but should be shaken for two or three minutes away from the fire, in order that, while it cools gradually, *all that fine aroma, on which depends the spirit, flavour, and excellence of coffee, may be imbibed,* instead of being lost by opening and emptying the roaster while any heat remains. As soon as it is cold, it must be poured into a glass bottle or canister, as before mentioned, and kept close stopped for use. Coffee wastes, in roasting, about two ounces in the pound.

Coffee undergoes important changes in the process of roasting. When it is roasted to a yellowish brown, it loses, according to Cadet, 12½ per cent. of its weight, and is in this state difficult to grind; when roasted to a chesnut-brown, it loses 18 per cent.; and when it becomes entirely black, though not at all carbonised, it has lost 23 per cent. When it loses more than 20 per cent. of its weight, in roasting, coffee is sure to be injured.

Bernier says, when he was at Cairo, where coffee is so much used, he was assured by the best judges, that there were only two people in that great city who understood how to prepare it in perfection. If it be under-roasted, its virtues will not be imparted, and in use it will load and oppress the stomach; if it be over-done, it will yield a flat, burnt and bitter taste, its virtues will be destroyed, and in use it will heat the body and act as an astringent.

Those who have not facilities for roasting the berries themselves, should employ one or other of the leading coffee-roasters of the metropolis, who, from their extensive premises, improved patented machinery, and great experience, may be safely entrusted with the preparation of the berry.

Messrs. James Collier and Son, of Foster-street, Bishopsgate, the oldest coffee-roasters in the metropolis, who have devoted much attention to the subject, have patented an improved apparatus for roasting, sifting, and cooling coffee.

The construction of their cylinder is quite different from any other, being made of a description of metal not before adopted for roasting coffee—the internal part of which is thickly cased with enamel.

The first object is cleanliness—the next is equally important, by preventing the coffee, while roasting, being impregnated with impurities of irony or sulphurous effluvia passing into the cylinder, which is not obviated by the general use of common plate-iron roasters worked over charcoal fires. Enamelled circular tubes pass through these cylinders, to convey an equal temperature of heat, and intersect the coffee while in revolving motion.

Dispersers (commonly called breakers) are so constructed and ingeniously arranged, as to sift the coffee while roasting, by which means all the acidity and rancid impurities of the raw coffee are emitted by evaporation, and the dust or flights removed from the cylinder through apertures, while the fine aromatic and nutritious qualities of the coffee are preserved. When the coffee is sufficiently roasted in these enamelled cylinders, it possesses that beautiful bright appearance so much approved. The hot coffee is then discharged into strong wire cylindrical coolers, which are immediately set to work in revolving motion by steam power, and, if necessary, by the application of forced atmospheric air dispersed into the revolving cooling cylinders, through the tubular perforated spindle.

By this new invention, the heat is extracted from the coffee, and it becomes sufficiently cold in about twenty minutes (at any period of the year), so that it is fit to grind for immediate use, or to be close packed for country orders.

The important advantages of roasted coffee being properly cooled, previous to grinding, closely packed in chests, or stored away into canisters, is obvious.

The essential or aromatic oil is retained in the berries, and the bright complexion of the coffee is preserved, without heating or discolouration.

Various Modes of making Coffee.

To make coffee equal to the French is very simple, and very easy; and, for the benefit of all good housewives, and all lovers of good coffee, I will state the manner in which it should be

done. First, procure the best coffee possible.
See that your cook does not *burn* it, but roast
it to the colour of a golden brown, and never
allow it to remain in its burnt or roasted state
for more than three or four days, as after that
time it will lose its strength.

Secondly, in lieu of the ancient method of *boiling* your coffee for an hour or more over a hot
fire, and then being obliged to settle it with such
rarities as fish-skins, egg-shells, and the like, procure a *biggen*, as it is termed, and make a distilla-
tion or decoction, by putting the coffee in the apart-
ment in which the strainer is, and turning thereon
boiling-hot water. Take care that the nose of the
coffee-pot has a stopper to prevent the steam from
escaping, and cover the top of your *biggen* immediately after having turned the water upon the
coffee, as it is a most important requisite to have
the steam confined. Judgment is also to be used
as to the amount of coffee required, and the
quantity of water to be used. The best coffee may
be spoiled by too much water being applied to it.
The coffee should be made very strong; and, if
strong enough, its colour will be quite black.

Lastly, having made your coffee of great
strength, do not use *hot water* to dilute it; but, in

lieu thereof, take boiling-hot milk, and weaken the coffee to your taste. By following these directions, you will have as fine a cup of coffee as can be made in any country.

The infusion of roasted coffee acquires a far superior taste, and is more concentrated, consequently, a much larger amount of beverage can be prepared from the same quantity of coffee, by adding to the boiling water, just before pouring it over the coffee, one grain of crystallised carbonate of soda for every cup, or two and a half grains for every half-ounce of coffee.

Infusions of Cold Water.

Dr. William Gregory, of Aberdeen, describes a very simple and cheap method of making the finest flavoured coffee, which is founded on the fact that cold water is capable of extracting all the pleasant and aromatic parts of roasted coffee.

The only apparatus required is a cylinder or percolator, and a few quart bottles. The percolator is a cylinder, 20 to 24 inches long, and 2 to 2½ inches wide, terminating below in a funnel, the neck of which enters a bottle placed to receive the coffee. The following is the method of using this simple apparatus :—The throat of the funnel

E

being lightly stopped with a clean bit of cotton wool, ¼ lb. of ground coffee is to be mixed up, in any convenient vessel, with so much cold water as thoroughly to moisten it and give it the consistence of thin porridge. When this has stood for an hour or so, the mass is introduced into the percolator by means of a wide filler. It immediately begins to drop into the bottle, and already the drops consist of a very strong infusion, nearly black. When the mass ceases to drop, the coffee is still impregnated with a very strong liquor. To obtain this, pour on gently through the upper end of the percolator as much cold water as fills it to the top. The pressure of the column of water forces out the liquid which is in the pores of the coffee, and fresh water takes its place. This in its turn becomes charged, though less strongly, with the soluble parts of the powder, and is, in its turn, displaced by the water above. At last, when the liquor which passes through (the percolator being filled up from time to time) becomes very pale, the operation may be stopped, as the liquid remaining in the powder is now too weak to repay the trouble of extracting it. The whole of the liquors which have passed through, and to collect which several bottles may have been required, are to be mixed together. If the directions above given be exactly followed, it will be found that, when made up, if necessary, to the bulk of six imperial pints, the resulting liquid is strong and perfectly clear coffee, of the most delicate flavour.

Should six pints have been passed through, the liquors, when mixed, are ready for use; but, if the filtered liquors amount, for example, to only four pints, two pints of water are to be added. This sometimes happens, because, from a variety of causes, the coffee is sooner exhausted in some experiments than in others. By the imperial pint, I understand a measure equal to 20 fluid ounces of water; or, in other words, a measure holding 1 lb. 4 oz. avoirdupois weight of water. Any one can make such a measure for himself, and mark it on a large quart bottle, which, being six times filled up to the mark, gives the above bulk of liquid. As this is 120 fluid ounces, and an ordinary tea-cup, moderately full, holds 4½ fluid ounces; or a breakfast-cup, moderately full, holds 6, the reader will perceive that, by this method, ½ lb. of coffee is made to yield twenty breakfast-cups or twenty-seven tea-cups of first-rate coffee.

It is hardly necessary to add, that if it be preferred to have it weaker, the same quantity may be

diluted to seven, eight, or even ten pints, and
thus be made to furnish thirty, forty, or more
breakfast-cups, the weakest of which will have a
better flavour than the trash which we are often
condemned to drink under the name of coffee.
In short, the strength is a matter of taste; and
the method above described enables every one to
please himself in this particular. None of the
liquor should be used till the operation is entirely
finished, for if some of the droppings are taken
away, the latter are apt to be lost, for want of a
strong infusion to mix them up with. As the
operation is a little tedious, lasting in all, three or
four days, it is necessary, as soon as the first portion is exhausted, to set a second in operation.
In this way, a supply is always at hand. The
coffee so made keeps perfectly as long as it may be
necessary to preserve it. For a small family, ½ lb.
is a good quantity to extract at one time; for a
large one, 1 lb. (of course in a large percolator 24
inches by 3 inches); and for single men, ¼ lb.,
in a cylinder 15 inches by 2. I ought not to
omit to add, that the exhausted coffee yields, when
boiled with water, so much soluble matter as to
furnish a considerable quantity of tolerable coffee,
not equal in flavour to the cold infusion, but far

from being disagreeable. When the cold infused coffee is to be used, it must of course be heated ; but it ought only to be brought to the boiling point and "not boiled," as boiling dissipates a great part of the flavour.

Another method is thus described by Dr. Ratier. Take four ounces of good coffee, properly roasted and ground. Dilute it in two glasses of cold water with a spoon. Let it steep all night, covering the vessel which contains it. Next day, pour this pap with care on fine linen placed in a glass funnel in a bottle. You have an extremely strong infusion, of which a single spoonful, poured in a cup of boiling milk, is sufficient to give the whole a delightful perfume. One part of this infusion, and two parts of pure water, put on the fire until it begins to boil, gives a coffee of a superb colour and perfect taste. It may indeed be conceived that coffee, treated cold, will not have parted with every portion of its aromatic principle. How can cold water draw from coffee all that can be obtained from it? I answer, yes! approved by experience. Indeed, I have tried the process related above with boiling and with cold water, and I have assured myself, by comparison, that the powder, drained by the cold water, and treated

then with boiling water, gave nothing but a water
slightly tinted with yellow, and devoid of odour
and flavour. It is, besides, proper to pass an equal
quantity of water to the first, over the grounds, in
order that the second water may serve for new
powder. There is thus both economy of fuel and
time, since the operation is done at once, and
constantly succeeds, if done in the same manner.
This process is not spoilt in the boiling, nor can
it frequently overflow, as in the apparatus called
Marize, and others, which answer the purpose
well, but are expensive to purchase, and require
repairs. As for myself, two small decanters of
glass, and a funnel of the same material, compose
all my apparatus. One of the decanters contains
the prepared coffee, and has a ground stopper.
The other, in which the funnel is placed, receives
the second water, and, in its turn, contains the
coffee, and thus both are used in succession; all
the care required is in passing a little water
through them at times. Every person who has
tasted my coffee, whether made with water or
milk, has found it of a superior quality. I am
astonished that so simple a process has not been
adopted. For the coffee houses it would ensure
the great advantage of always having coffee ready

made, not by adding water to the milk, which contains enough already, or making the coffee from hand to mouth, but in a manner by which none of the qualities sought for by true amateurs are lost.

Messrs. Smith, of Duke-street, Edinburgh, suggest the following plan of making coffee:—

We make use of a pneumatic percolating coffee-pot, many excellent forms of which have been for a considerable time before the public; but, instead of passing all the water required for the diet, we place upon the strainer as much fresh roasted coffee as will fill the pot; then pour over the coffee as much boiling water as will completely moisten it, and let it stand thus for about an hour, so as to render the soluble part of the coffee more easily exhausted afterwards. We then fill up the pot with boiling water, or a quantity equal in bulk to the coffee used; and, as soon as this is done, withdraw the air from beneath the strainer; and when, by the pressure of external air, the water has been completely pushed through, pour on a fresh quantity of boiling water equal to the first, and pass it through the coffee in the same way. In like manner, we make use of at least a third water; and when the last has passed through, the united liquids are

poured into a bottle, and carefully corked. In this
state it is always ready for use, and requires merely
in the proportion of a few tea-spoonsful, more or
less, according to taste, to be mixed with a cup of
boiling water or boiling milk, to produce an exceedingly grateful and delicious drink, retaining quite
unimpaired the peculiar aroma of the coffee; and
as the strainer retains even the finest solid particles, the liquid is perfectly dry and transparent, and
of course quite free of grounds. As the coffee on
the strainer is not yet quite exhausted, two or three
additional waters may be passed through, and,
united together, may be drank without dilution.

This process is founded on the fact that there is a
limit to the solvent power of water and other liquids,
and that they will not take up more than a certain quantity of the soluble part of any substance
presented to their action; and when they have
taken up this quantity, they cannot, by any means,
under ordinary conditions, be made to take up any
more, and are therefore said to be saturated; and
it is found that the nearer the liquid approaches
this state, the act of solution goes on the more
slowly. In the usual way of making infusions,
such as those of coffee or tea, the process goes
on very slowly, notwithstanding the large propor-

tion of water to the solid matter; for, although the water in immediate contact with this soon becomes saturated; yet, in consequence of this very circumstance, it becomes of greater specific gravity, or heavier than the rest of the liquid, and, by reason of this, remains in the mass at the bottom; and in this way excludes the rest of the liquid which has not yet exerted its solvent power. The agitation or currents resulting from the ordinary heat applied, remedy this in part, but only in part. Another objection connected with the ordinary method of infusion is, that, as the infusion advances, the liquid becomes more and more saturated; and, as a sure consequence of this, as has been already explained, the process goes on in the same proportion the more slowly. In the process of percolation, the liquid approaches the solid with its full solvent power, becomes saturated; and immediately passing out of the way, gives place to a fresh portion of the solvent. In this way, the substance can, by proper care, be exhausted of its soluble parts with an exceedingly small quantity of fluid, and a very concentrated solution obtained.

All that is required for the process is a hollow cylinder, open at top and bottom, of common tinplate, wood, earthenware, &c., having a lip or groove at one end, over which end a piece of linen or calico must be tightly tied for a bottom, and the coffee placed upon this, which must be treated successively with water, as before explained; the liquid, as it drops through the strainer, being received by a convenient vessel placed beneath, and the cylinder being supported over this, either by means of three or four arms attached to the outside, resting on the edge of the vessel or the cylinder, by a strong cord, may be suspended above the vessel. The only difference between this method and that where a pneumatic apparatus is used, is that a longer time is required; but, as no more attention is necessary, than merely to add water when the previous quantity is passed through, this is of little moment. An excellent cylinder for the purpose could be easily obtained by knocking the bottom from a common jelly-pot.

I have tried (says Benson Hill, in his " Epicure's Almanac") nearly every method of preparing this Arabian beverage, and find, after all, that there is no surer way of having coffee clear and strong, than pursuing the plan here given. Beat up an egg—two for a large pot—and mix it well with the coffee, till you have formed it into a ball; fill the pot with *cold* water, allowing room enough to put in the ingredients; let it simmer very gently for an hour, but do not think of stirring it, on any account; just before it is required, put the pot on the fire, and warm it well; but, as you value the true aroma, take care that it does not boil. Pour it off gently, and you will have as pure and strong an extract of the Indian berry as you can desire. Use white sugar-candy in powder in preference to sugar; cream, if attainable; if not, boiled milk.

Here is a receipe for making " Coffee Royal," by a sportsman. *Gloria* is a redolent mixture of coffee, loaf sugar (sugar-candy is better), and cognac. To half a cupful of strong coffee, add four large lumps of sugar; then pour over the back of your tea-spoon, with a steady hand, about as much fine old cognac as you have of coffee: the spirit will of course float on the coffee, and great care must be taken that the two fluids mix not; then light the brandy, and, when the evil spirit has evaporated, stir the beverage, and you will have one of the most delicious liqueurs imaginable; and, independently of its exhilarating powers, it will be found to possess digestive qualities in no ordinary degree; and I strongly recommend this fascinating compound to all dyspeptic people.

Dr. Roques' receipt for a *café à la crême frappé de glace*. It is a delicious breakfast during the summer heats. " Make a strong infusion of Mocha or Bourbon coffee; put it into a porcelain bowl, sugar it properly, and add to it an equal portion of boiled milk, or one-third the quantity of rich cream. Surround the bowl with pounded ice." Dr. Bonnafous, of Perpignan, recommended this beverage to such persons as had lost their appetite, or who experienced general debility.

Coffee as made in France.

France is most justly celebrated as the country where coffee is prepared in the most perfect way. The French are of a volatile disposition, and require less of what tends to create an unnatural excitement of the nervous system, than something exhilarating to maintain the natural buoyancy of their spirits. Coffee has been found to possess those qualities in an eminent degree; and the consequence is, that an amazing number of houses have been established in Paris, and other large towns in France, solely for its sale. From the competition among the different *cafés*, every effort is used to excel in making it, which partly accounts for the excellence of French coffee.

The quality of the raw material is no better in France than in England. There is no reason whatever, except our general ignorance of the subject, why coffee should not be brought to the table in as high perfection in this country as in any part of the world.

In Paris one kind of coffee is scarcely ever used alone ; three, four, or five sorts, mixed together, are preferred to any one kind by itself; and the fine beverage that is made there is, in a great measure, owing to the skill with which these various descriptions of coffee are proportioned to each other.

Coffee, as used on the Continent, serves the double purpose of an agreeable tonic and an ex-hilarating beverage. A cup of coffee strengthens and exhilarates both the mental and bodily facul-ties; and nothing can be more refreshing, either to the studious or the laborious, than a cup of good coffee. This fact we have had practically and powerfully illustrated by Napoleon Bonaparte, whose buoyancy of mind and energies, intellectual and physical, were perhaps never surpassed by any man. He abstained from the use of spirituous liquors, but drank coffee at all hours of the day, to revive his spirits and invigorate his body.

The following is given as the mode in which he directed his coffee to be prepared:—

For three or four persons, two ounces of recently burnt and ground coffee are put into an empty coffee-pot of the ordinary kind, with a small piece of isinglass; this is held over the fire, and shaken by the hand, so as to prevent the burning of the coffee. When a smoke is seen to issue from the pot at the boiling point, milk is poured upon it in a sufficient quantity to supply six breakfast-cups, in the proportion of one-third of coffee to two-thirds of milk. The coffee-pot is taken from the fire before the water is added, but, being heated, the coffee boils gently as the pot is held in the hand. The ebullition is sufficient to bring out all the fine properties of the coffee without carrying off the aroma. A cup is then poured out and returned again to the pot, to allow the powder to precipitate; and in two or three minutes, the coffee is perfectly clear, and is used with boiling milk. Some of the best families in Paris now adopt this plan, which is certainly superior to many now in use.

A writer in " Bentley's Miscellany" gives a gra-

phic description of the customs of the French in
the consumption of this beverage. " Coffee," he
observes, " is to the Frenchman what tea is to the
Englishman, beer to the German, *eau de vie* to the
Russian, opium to the Turk, or chocolate to the
Spaniard. Men, women, and children of all grades
and professions drink coffee in Paris. In the morning, it is served up under the aromatic name of
café au lait; in the evening, it is universally taken
as *café noir.* After one of Vefour's magnificent
repasts, it enters your stomach in the character of
a settler. It leaves you volatile, nimble and quick;
and over it might be justly poured those pleasant
compliments which Falstaff bestowed on sherries
(sack). The garçon, at your call for a *demi-tasse*,
has placed before you a snowy cup and saucer,
three lumps of sugar, and a *petit verre.* He
ventured the *petit verre*, inferring, from your
ruddy English face, that you liked *liqueur.* Another garçon now appears ; in his right hand is a
huge silver pot, and in his left, another of the
same material, uncovered : the former contains
coffee—the latter, cream. You reject cream, and
thereupon the garçon pours out of the former until
your cup—aye, and almost the saucer—actually
overflows. There is hardly space for the three

lumps, and yet you must contrive, somehow, to insert them; or that *café noir—black* it may indeed be called—will, in its concentrated state, be quite unmanageable; but, when thus sweetly tempered, it becomes the finest beverage in the whole world. It agreeably affects several senses. Its liquid pleases all the gustatory nerves, its savour ascends to rejoice the olfactory, and even your eye is delighted with those dark, transparent, and sparkling hues, through which your silver spoon perpetually shines. You pronounce French coffee the only coffee. In a few moments its miracles begin to be wrought: you feel *spirituel*, amiable, and conversational.

Delille's fine lines rush into your memory :—

' *Et je crois du génie éprouvant le reveil,*
    Boire dans chaque goutte un rayon du soleil.' "

M. Soyer's Receipt (and who can doubt his authority) is as follows :—Put two ounces of ground coffee into a stewpan, which set upon the fire, stirring the powder round with a spoon until quite hot; then pour over a pint of boiling water; cover it closely for five minutes, pass it through a cloth, warm again, and serve.

The foregoing proportions, he adds, would make

coffee good enough for any person; but more or less coffee could be used, if required. The cloth through which it is passed should be immediately washed, and put by for the next occasion. A hundred cups of coffee could be made as here directed in half an hour, by procuring a pan sufficiently large, and using the proper proportions of coffee and water, passing it afterwards through a large cloth or jelly-bag.

White Coffee is made after the following manner: —Put two ounces of unground coffee, slightly roasted, into a clean stewpan, which set upon a moderate fire, slowly warming the coffee through, shaking the stewpan round every half-minute; when very hot, which you will perceive by the smoke arising from it, pour over half a pint of boiling water; cover the stewpan well, and let it infuse by the side of the fire for fifteen minutes; then add half a pint of boiling-hot milk; pass the coffee through a small, fine sieve, into the coffee-pot or jug, and serve with white sugar-candy or crystallised sugar. It is a great novelty and an agreeable change; but if, by neglect, you let the coffee get black, or the least burnt, do not attempt to make use of it; it should only be sufficiently charred to break easily in a mortar, if required.

Here is *another of Soyer's Receipts;* for making
coffee with a filter.—To make a quart, first put a
pint of boiling water in the filter, to warm it, which
pour away; then put a quarter of a pound of
ground coffee upon the filter, and upon which put
the presser and the grating lightly; pour over half
a pint of boiling water; let it stand three or four
minutes; then pour over a pint and a half more
boiling water; when well passed through, pour it
into a clear stewpan; which set at the corner of
the fire until a light scum arises, but not boiling;
pour it again through the filter; and, when well
drained through, pour into the coffee-pot, and
serve with hot milk, or a little cream, sepa-
rately.—*Soyer's ' Menagère.'*

Another and more economical way is to proceed
as in the last described receipt, but drain the
coffee through once only, and serve; after which,
pour another quart of boiling water over the coffee
grounds, which, when drained through, reserve,
and boil up for the next coffee you make, using it
instead of water; use an ounce less coffee.

*To make Coffee in the French fashion—Café au
lait.*—To a pint of coffee, made according to the
plan of M. Soyer, before given, add a pint of
boiling milk; warm both together until nearly

boiling, and serve. The French never use it in any other way for breakfast.

Coffee Milk.—Boil a dessert-spoonful of ground coffee in nearly a pint of milk a quarter of an hour; then put into it a shaving or two of isinglass, to clear it; let it boil a few minutes, and set it on the side of the fire to fine. This is very suitable for a weak stomach.

Coffee as drank in Turkey.

Coffee is the universal and almost only beverage of the Turks, the Arabs, and the Eastern nations, and is considered by them as the special gift of Heaven. The Persians, who appreciate highly its delicious virtues, venerate it from the romantic notion, that it was first invented and brewed by the angel Gabriel, to restore Mahomet's decayed moisture, which it did effectually.

The Turks prepare their coffee in a most simple manner. A small vessel, containing about a wine-glass of water, is placed on the fire; and, when boiling, a tea-spoonful of ground coffee is put into it, stirred up, and suffered to boil and bubble a few seconds longer, when it is poured (grounds and all) into a cup about the size of an egg-shell, encased in gold or silver filigree work, to protect the finger from the heat; and the liquid, in its scalding, black, thick, and troubled state, is imbibed with the greatest relish. Like smoking, this must be quite an acquired taste.

People of all classes in Constantinople use these drinks. A good cup of strong coffee may be had for a farthing, and a glass of sherbet for little more. Their coffee is made in a simple, easy manner, and most expeditiously. When a single cup is called for, the attendant in the coffee-house pours hot water into a little copper pan, or rather pot; puts it over a charcoal fire for an instant, to make it boil; then adds a proportion of well-ground or pounded coffee, either alone or mixed with sugar; returns it again to the fire, to boil for an instant; and the coffee is made. It is poured, boiling-hot, into a small porcelain cup, and handed to the customer; the coarser grounds quickly subside in a few seconds, whilst cooling down to the drinking-point. Disagreeable at first, a taste for this strong unclarified coffee is soon acquired. It is an excellent and safe substitute for a dram.

Major Skinner, in his " Overland Journey to India," says, "It is astonishing what effect the

smallest portion of the strong coffee made by the
Arabs has ; no greater stimulus is required in the
longest and most arduous journeys. It is universal throughout the East ; but more used by the
Arabs of the desert than by any other class.
They will go without food for twenty-four hours, if
they can but have recourse to the little dram of
coffee, which, from the small compass in which
they carry the apparatus, and the readiness with
which it is made, they can always command. I can
vouch for both its strengthening and exhilarating
effects."

The khans and meerzas of Bebuhan are considerable consumers of coffee ; but not after the
fashion of Turks, Arabs, or Europeans. It is with
them a kind of *bon-bon*, eaten in a powdered and
roasted state, without having had any connection
with hot water. " When Meer Goolam Hussein
called on me (says the author of a ' Pilgrimage
through Persia'), he was always accompanied by his
coffee-bearer, who carried about the fragrant berry
in a snuff-box, and handed it frequently to the com
pany present. The first time it was brought to me,
deceived by its colour and quality, and strengthened
in the delusion by its singular repository, I took a
pinch of the coffee, and applied it to my nose,

amidst the roars of laughter and looks of surprise of all the party."

System of Cultivating the Coffee Tree.

The coffee tree is rather a tender plant, until it grows to maturity. It would rise to the height of fourteen or fifteen feet, if permitted; but it is bad management to allow it to grow to more than four or five feet. This tree bears berries at three years old, but comes to maturity at five. It will grow in almost any soil. Although the tree affords no return to the planter for nearly four years, yet, after that time, with little or no labour bestowed on it, it will yield two crops a year. One gathering takes place in May or June, and the other in October or the beginning of November. The berries in our colonies are often plucked of unequal ripeness, which must greatly injure the quality of the coffee. It is true, when the coffee is washed, the berries which float on the water are separated from the others; but they are only those of the worst quality, or broken pieces, while the half-ripe beans remain at the bottom with the best. Now, in the description given of the method of gathering coffee in Arabia, it is said the tree is suffered to grow to its natural height, and the berries are

gathered by shaking the tree, and making them
fall on mats placed for the purpose. By this way,
the Arabians gather only the beans perfectly ripe
at the time, and which must give the coffee a more
delicate flavour.

A coffee plantation is a business rather of plea-
sure than of toil; and forms the most delightful of
all tropical cultivation. Nothing can exceed the
beauty of the walks planted with coffee trees, from
their pyramidical shape, and from their glossy,
dark green leaves shining with great brightness,
amongst which are hanging the scarlet-coloured
berries.

The aspect of a coffee plantation during the
period of flowering, which does not last longer than
one or two days, is very interesting. In one night,
the blossoms expand themselves so profusely, as to
present the same appearance which is sometimes
witnessed in England, when a casual snow-storm at
the close of autumn has loaded the trees, while
still furnished with their full complement of
foliage.

In most countries, coffee is the produce of up-
land and mountainous regions—the driest climates
producing the best berries; but there is no valid
reason for the preference of elevated ranges; for,

by proper culture, the tree flourishes, and fruits equally well in well drained plains.

The seeds are known to be sufficiently ripe when they assume a dark red or nearly a black colour, and in this state their pulpy bark begins to shrivel. When the berry is allowed to become over ripe, it is of a dark purple colour, and filled with a sweet pulp. If not then gathered, they will drop from the trees. The produce of a good tree is from one and a half to two pounds of berries. Each bushel of ripe berries will yield about ten pounds' weight of merchantable coffee. The tree flourishes best in countries in which the thermometer does not fall below 55°.

The culture of coffee is declining in all our West Indian colonies, in consequence of the abolition of slavery. In 1828, about thirty millions of pounds were shipped from the British West India Colonies. Not one-eighth of that quantity is now exported.

Coffee, by law, cannot be imported in packages of less than 100 lbs. nett weight. It is usually brought to this country either in bags or casks.

LONDON:
PRINTED BY EFFINGHAM WILSON, ROYAL EXCHANGE.